Love & Friendship
Quilted Pillows

Great for gifts to celebrate love and friendship, these six appliqué pillows offer lots of fun free-motion quilting. You'll want some for your home, too.

BLESS YOUR HEART

Finished Size: 24$\frac{1}{2}$" x 24$\frac{1}{2}$" (62 x 62 cm)

SHOPPING LIST

Yardage is based on 43"/44" (109 cm/112 cm) wide fabric with a usable width of 40" (102 cm).

☐ Scraps of assorted olive, gold, burgundy, pink, and blue prints

☐ Scraps [at least 12" x 12" (30 x 30 cm) *each*] of 5 tan or gold prints

☐ $\frac{1}{4}$ yd (23 cm) of light olive checked print

☐ Approximately $\frac{1}{4}$ yd (23 cm) of floral motif print*

☐ $\frac{1}{4}$ yd (23 cm) of burgundy polka dot print

☐ $\frac{7}{8}$ yd (80 cm) of fabric for pillow back

☐ 2$\frac{1}{2}$ yds (2.3 m) of muslin

You will also need:

☐ 29$\frac{1}{2}$" x 29$\frac{1}{2}$" (75 x 75 cm) square of batting

☐ Polyester fiberfill

☐ Paper-backed fusible web

☐ Tracing paper

☐ Stabilizer

☐ Hot-iron transfer pen

☐ Brown embroidery floss

☐ Assorted buttons

*You will need to cut 4 hearts [approximately 5$\frac{1}{2}$" x 6" (14 x 15 cm)] centering floral motifs.

CUTTING OUT THE PIECES

*Follow **Rotary Cutting**, page 38, to cut pieces. Measurements listed include seam allowances. Follow **Preparing Fusible Appliqués**, page 39, to cut appliqués. Appliqué patterns do not include seam allowance and are reversed.*

From scraps of olive, gold, burgundy, pink, and blue prints:
• Cut 36 **small squares** 3" x 3".

From scraps of tan or gold prints:
• Cut 5 **large squares** 10" x 10".

From light olive checked print:
• Cut 2 **top/bottom borders** 1$\frac{3}{4}$" x 25$\frac{1}{2}$".
• Cut 2 **side borders** 1$\frac{3}{4}$" x 23".

From floral motif print:
• Centering floral motif, cut 4 **small heart** appliqués using pattern on page 5.

From burgundy polka dot print:
• Cut 5 **large heart** appliqués using pattern on page 5.

From fabric for pillow back:
• Cut 2 rectangles 16" x 25$\frac{1}{2}$" for **pillow back**.

From muslin:
• Cut 1 **large muslin square** 29$\frac{1}{2}$" x 29$\frac{1}{2}$".
• Cut 2 **small muslin squares** 25$\frac{1}{2}$" x 25$\frac{1}{2}$".

MAKING THE PILLOW

*Follow **Piecing**, page 38, **Pressing**, page 39, and **Decorative Stitch Appliqué**, page 39, to make pillow top. Use $\frac{1}{4}$" seam allowances unless otherwise indicated. Our pillow features machine Blanket Stitch appliqué. Hand embroidered Blanket Stitch with 2 strands of embroidery floss may be substituted. **Hand Stitches** are shown on pages 42-43.*

1. Appliqué **large heart** for Center Block to 1 **large square**. Using tracing paper and hot-iron transfer pen and centering words in area cut out of heart, transfer words, page 5, to large square. Backstitch words using 2 strands of brown floss to complete **Center Block**. Trim Center Block to 8" x 8".

Center Block

2. Centering **small heart** on top of **large heart**, fuse hearts to 1 **large square**; appliqué. Repeat (slightly turning hearts as desired) to make 4 **Corner Blocks**. Trim Corner Blocks to 8" x 8".

Corner Block (make 4)

3. Sew 3 **small squares** together to make **Unit 1**. Make 12 Unit 1's.

Unit 1 (make 12)

4. Sew 3 **Unit 1's** together to complete **Nine-Patch Block**. Make 4 Nine-Patch Blocks.

Nine-Patch Block (make 4)

5. Sew 2 **Corner Blocks** and 1 **Nine-Patch Block** together to make **Row A**. Make 2 Row A's.

Row A (make 2)

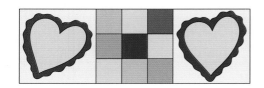

6. Sew **Center Block** and 2 **Nine-Patch Blocks** together to make **Row B**.

Row B

7. Sew **Rows** together to make center section of pillow top.

8. Sew **side**, **top**, then **bottom borders** to center section to complete **pillow top**.

9. Layer **large muslin square**, batting, and pillow top (right side up and centered). Follow **Quilting**, page 41, to baste and quilt as desired. Our pillow has crosshatching in the nine-patch blocks and decorative quilting in the heart blocks and border.

10. Tie buttons to pillow top using 6 strands of brown floss. Trim batting and large muslin square even with edges of pillow top.

11. On each **pillow back** rectangle, press 1 *long* edge ¹/₄" to the wrong side; press ¹/₄" to the wrong side again and stitch in place.

12. Overlap hemmed edges of pillow back rectangles, right sides facing up, to form 25¹/₂" x 25¹/₂" square. Baste pillow back rectangles together at overlap.

13. With right sides facing, pin pillow top and pillow back together. Sew around pillow using ¹/₂" **seam allowance**. Remove basting, turn, and press.

14. To make pillow form, sew 2 **small muslin squares** together using ¹/₂" **seam allowance** and leaving opening for turning. Clip corners, turn, and press. Fill with fiberfill; sew opening closed. Insert pillow form in pillow.

Pillow Top Diagram

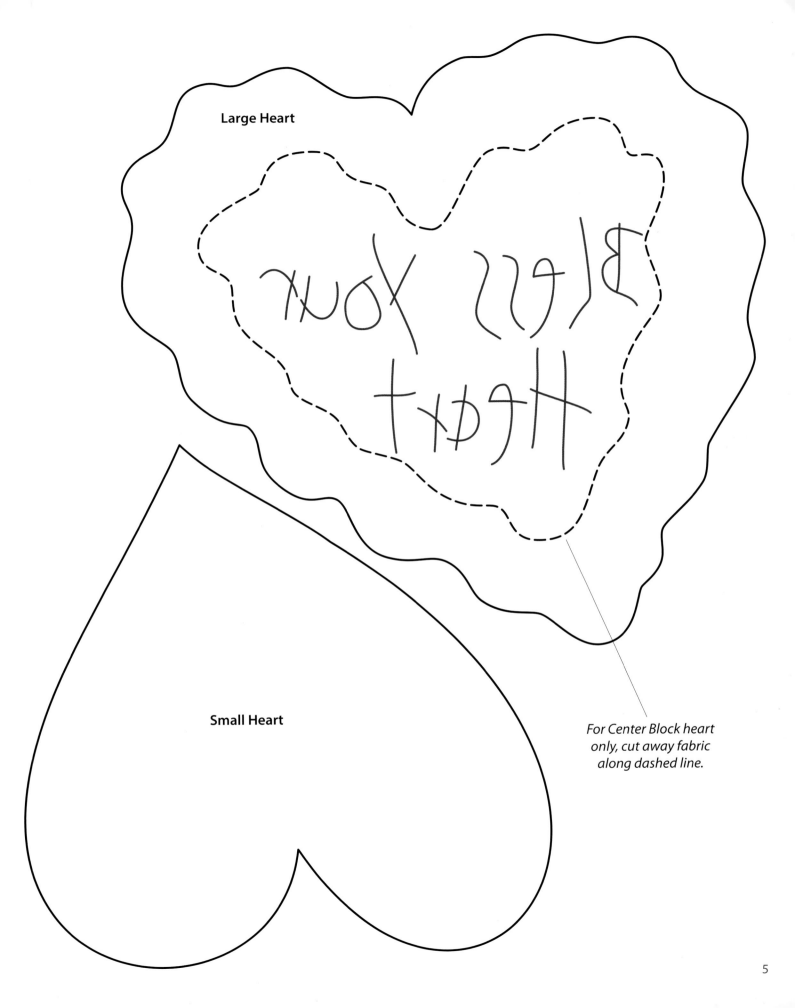

Large Heart

Small Heart

For Center Block heart only, cut away fabric along dashed line.

FRIENDSHIP

Finished Size: 24" x 17" (61 x 43 cm)

SHOPPING LIST

Yardage is based on 43"/44" (109 cm/112 cm) wide fabric with a usable width of 40" (102 cm).

- ☐ ³/₈ yd (34 cm) of cream print
- ☐ ¹/₈ yd (11 cm) *each of* 8 assorted prints
- ☐ ¹/₄ yd (23 cm) of dark blue polka dot print
- ☐ Scrap of gold print #1
- ☐ Scrap of gold print #2
- ☐ ⁵/₈ yd (57 cm) of fabric for pillow back
- ☐ 1¹/₂ yds (1.4 m) of muslin

You will also need:

- ☐ 29" x 22" (74 x 56 cm) piece of batting
- ☐ Polyester fiberfill
- ☐ Paper-backed fusible web
- ☐ Stabilizer
- ☐ Tracing paper
- ☐ Hot-iron transfer pen
- ☐ Brown embroidery floss
- ☐ Assorted novelty buttons

CUTTING OUT THE PIECES

*Follow **Rotary Cutting**, page 38, to cut pieces. Measurements listed include seam allowances. Follow **Preparing Fusible Appliqués**, page 39, to cut appliqués. Appliqué patterns do not include seam allowance and are reversed.*

From cream print:

- Cut 1 **rectangle** 16¹/₂" x 9¹/₂".

From assorted prints:

- Cut 8 strips (1 from each fabric) of varying widths (2¹/₂" - 4"). Cut across each strip at 4³/₄" intervals to make **border rectangles**.

From dark blue polka dot print:

- Cut 2 **long faux sashing** appliqués 25" long using pattern on page 10, repeating pattern as necessary.
- Cut 2 **short faux sashing** appliqués 18" long using pattern on page 10, repeating pattern as necessary.

From gold print #1:

- Cut 1 **rays** appliqué using pattern on page 9.

From gold print #2:

- Cut 1 **sun** appliqué using pattern on page 9.

From fabric for pillow back:

- Cut 2 rectangles 15¹/₂" x 18" for **pillow back**.

From muslin:

- Cut 1 **large muslin rectangle** 29" x 22".
- Cut 2 **small muslin rectangles** 25" x 18".

As the sunshine
warms the earth and makes
the flowers grow
your friendship warms my
heart xxx I just wanted you to know

MAKING THE PILLOW

*Follow **Piecing**, page 38, **Pressing**, page 39, and **Decorative Stitch Appliqué**, page 39, to make pillow top. Use ¹/₄" seam allowances unless otherwise indicated. Our pillow features machine Blanket Stitch appliqué. Hand embroidered Blanket Stitch with 2 strands of embroidery floss may be substituted. **Hand Stitches** are shown on pages 42-43.*

1. Sew enough **border rectangles** together to make 2 top/bottom borders 4³/₄" x 16¹/₂" and 2 side borders 4³/₄" x 18".

Top/Bottom Border (make 2)

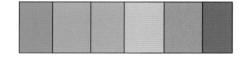

Side Border (make 2)

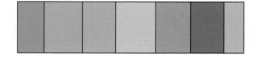

2. Sew **top, bottom,** then **side borders** to **rectangle**.

3. Center 1 **long faux sashing** on seam between rectangle and top border; fuse and appliqué. Repeat with remaining long faux sashing on seam between rectangle and bottom border.

4. Repeat Step 3, appliquéing **short faux sashings** between rectangle and side borders.

5. Referring to photo, page 7, and Pillow Top Diagram for placement, fuse and appliqué **rays** and **sun** to pillow top. **(Note:** *Be sure to allow for* ¹/₂" *seam allowance at pillow top edges.)*

6. Using tracing paper and hot-iron transfer pen, transfer words, pages 10-11, to rectangle. Backstitch words using 3 strands of brown floss.

7. Layer **large muslin rectangle**, batting, and pillow top (right side up and centered). Follow **Quilting**, page 41, to baste and quilt as desired. Our pillow has decorative quilting around the words and in the borders.

8. Sew buttons to pillow top. Trim batting and large muslin rectangle even with edges of pillow top.

9. On each **pillow back** rectangle, press 1 **long** edge ¹/₄" to the wrong side; press ¹/₄" to the wrong side again and stitch in place.

10. Overlap hemmed edges of pillow back rectangles, right sides facing up, to form 25" x 18" rectangle. Baste pillow back rectangles together at overlap.

11. With right sides facing, pin pillow top and pillow back together. Sew around pillow using ¹/₂" **seam allowance**. Remove basting, turn, and press.

12. To make pillow form, sew 2 **small muslin rectangles** together using ¹/₂" **seam allowance** and leaving opening for turning. Clip corners, turn and press. Fill with fiberfill; sew opening closed. Insert pillow form in pillow.

Pillow Top Diagram

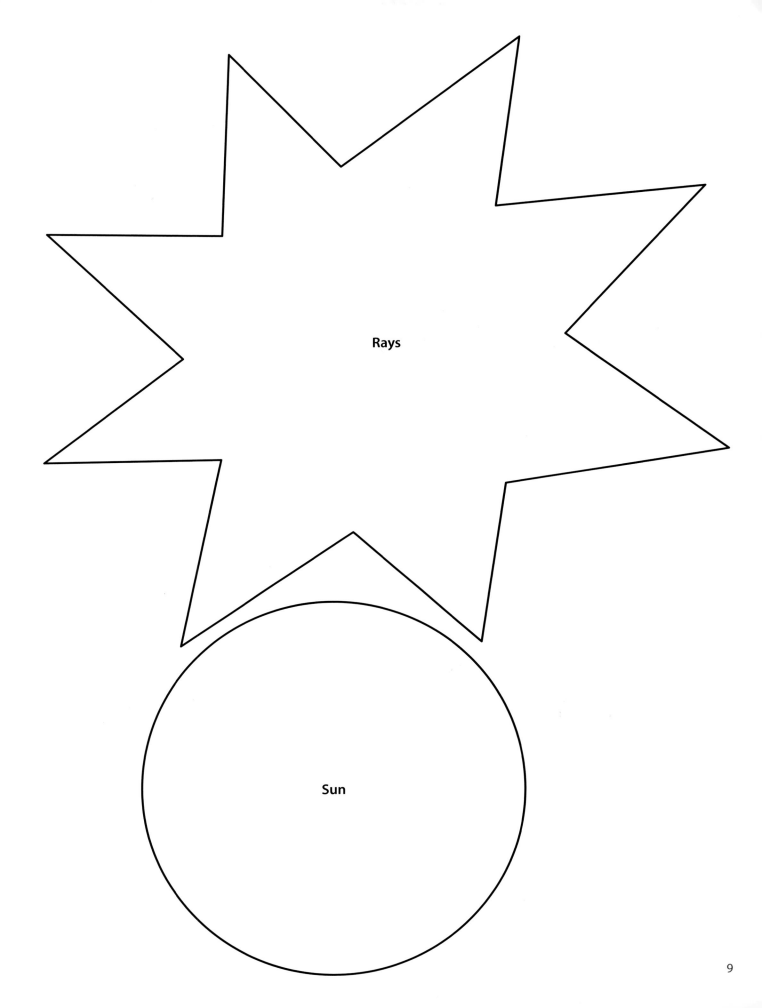

Rays

Sun

Faux Sashing

Grey area indicates overlap.

BRAND NEW HEART

Finished Size: 19" x 17" (48 x 43 cm)

SHOPPING LIST

*Yardage is based on 43"/44"
(109 cm/112 cm) wide fabric with
a usable width of 40" (102 cm).*

- ☐ $1/2$ yd (46 cm) of cream print
- ☐ $1/8$ yd (11 cm) of black solid
- ☐ $1/4$ yd (23 cm) of gold print
- ☐ Scraps of assorted prints for heart
- ☐ $5/8$ yd (57 cm) of fabric for pillow back
- ☐ $1^3/8$ yds (1.3 m) of muslin

You will also need:

- ☐ 24" x 22" (61 x 56 cm) piece of batting
- ☐ Polyester fiberfill
- ☐ Paper-backed fusible web
- ☐ Stabilizer
- ☐ Tracing paper
- ☐ Water- or air-soluble fabric pen
- ☐ Hot-iron transfer pen
- ☐ Black embroidery floss
- ☐ Assorted novelty buttons
- ☐ Fine-point marker

CUTTING OUT THE PIECES

*Follow **Rotary Cutting**, page 38, to cut
pieces. Measurements listed include
seam allowances.*

From cream print:

- Cut 1 **large rectangle** $16^1/2$" x $14^1/2$".

From black solid:

- Cut 2 **top/bottom inner borders** 1" x $14^1/2$".
- Cut 2 **side inner borders** 1" x $13^1/2$".

From gold print:

- Cut 2 **top/bottom outer borders** $2^3/4$" x $15^1/2$".
- Cut 2 **side outer borders** $2^3/4$" x 18".

From fabric for pillow back:

- Cut 2 rectangles 13" x 18" for **pillow back.**

From muslin:

- Cut 2 **small muslin rectangles** 20" x 18".
- Cut 1 **large muslin rectangle** 24" x 22".

MAKING PAPER-PIECED APPLIQUÉ HEART

1. Using fine-point marker, trace **pieced heart** pattern, page 18, onto tracing paper.

2. Rough cut a piece of assorted print for heart at least ¹/₂" larger on all sides than area 1 on traced pattern (foundation). Completely cover area 1 of foundation with fabric, wrong sides together (**Fig. 1**). Pin fabric in place. Fold foundation on line between area 1 and area 2. Trim fabric ¹/₄" from fold (**Fig. 2**). Unfold foundation.

Fig. 1

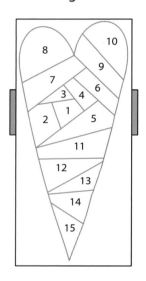

Fig. 2

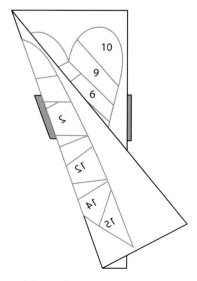

3. Rough cut a piece of another assorted print in the same manner for area 2 on foundation. Match right sides and align 1 edge of piece #2 with trimmed edge of piece #1. (**Fig. 3**). Turn foundation over to front and pin.

Fig. 3

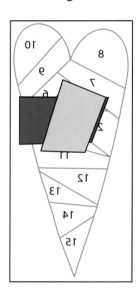

4. Sew along drawn line between areas 1 and 2, extending sewing a few stitches beyond beginning and ending of line (**Fig. 4**).

Fig. 4

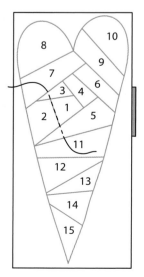

5. Open out piece #2; press. Pin piece #2 to foundation (**Fig. 5**). Fold foundation on line between area 2 and 3. Trim fabric ¹/₄" from fold. Unfold foundation.

Fig. 5

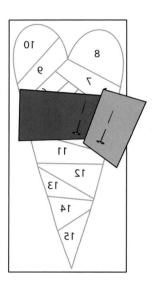

6. Repeat Steps 2-5, adding pieces in numerical order. When adding piece #9, stitch to the inner point of heart *exactly*, and backstitch to reinforce. Add remaining pieces until the foundation is covered. Carefully remove paper foundation.

7. Trace heart shape from **pieced heart** pattern onto paper side of fusible web. Follow manufacturer's instructions to fuse web to wrong side of pieced fabric heart. Cut along traced lines of heart outline.

MAKING THE PILLOW

*Follow **Piecing**, page 38, **Pressing**, page 39, and **Decorative Stitch Appliqué**, page 39, to make pillow top. Use ¹/₄" seam allowances unless otherwise indicated. Our pillow features machine Blanket Stitch appliqué. Hand embroidered Blanket Stitch with 2 strands of embroidery floss may be substituted. **Hand Stitches** are shown on pages 42-43.*

1. Using water- or air-soluble fabric pen, lightly mark a 14" x 12" rectangle in center of **large rectangle**. *(This will be the finished size of rectangle. Embroidery and appliqué should fit within drawn rectangle.)* Referring to photo, page 13, and **Pillow Top Diagram**, fuse and appliqué heart to large rectangle.

2. Using 2 strands of black floss, add a Running Stitch ¹/₄" from outside edge of heart appliqué.

3. Using tracing paper and hot-iron transfer pen, transfer words, pages 16-17, to large rectangle. Backstitch words using 2 strands of black floss. Trim large rectangle to 14¹/₂" x 12¹/₂" (¹/₄" outside drawn rectangle).

4. Sew **top**, **bottom**, then **side inner borders** to large rectangle. Repeat to add **outer borders**.

5. Layer **large muslin rectangle**, batting, and pillow top (right side up and centered). Follow **Quilting**, page 41, to baste and quilt as desired. Our pillow is machine quilted. It has stipple quilting around words and heart and in the borders. The heart pieces are quilted in the ditch.

6. Tie buttons onto pillow top using 6 strands of black floss. Trim batting and large muslin rectangle even with edges of pillow top.

7. On each **pillow back** rectangle, press 1 *long* edge ¹/₄" to the wrong side; press ¹/₄" to the wrong side again and stitch in place.

8. Overlap hemmed edges of pillow back rectangles, right sides facing up, to form 20" x 18" rectangle. Baste pillow back rectangles together at overlap.

9. Pin pillow top and pillow back together, right sides facing. Sew around pillow using ¹/₂" **seam allowance**. Remove basting, turn, and press.

10. To make pillow form, sew 2 **small muslin rectangles** together using ¹/₂" **seam allowance** and leaving opening for turning. Clip corners, turn, and press. Fill with fiberfill; sew opening closed. Insert pillow form in pillow.

Pillow Top Diagram

take the pieces
that's come apart
all

Heart new

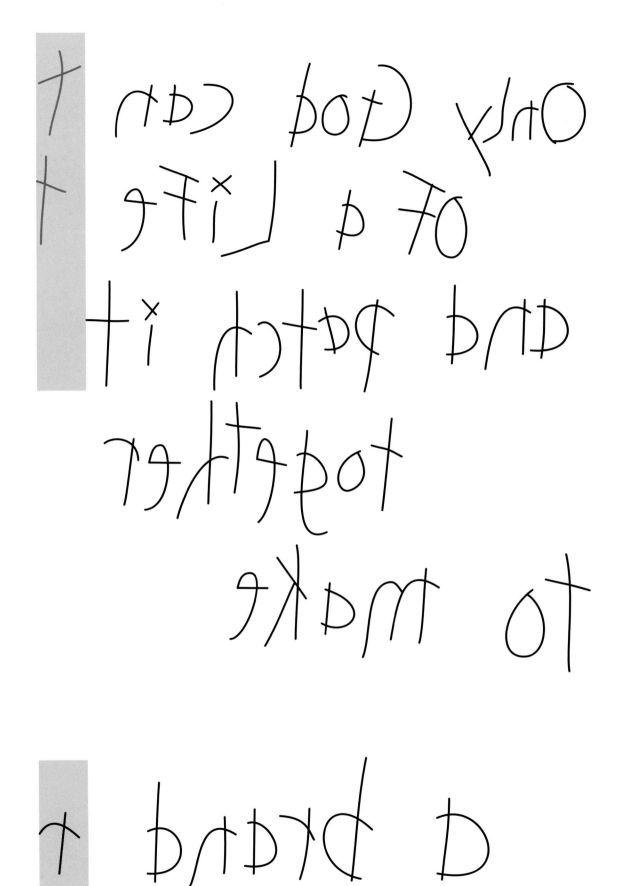

Grey areas indicate overlap.

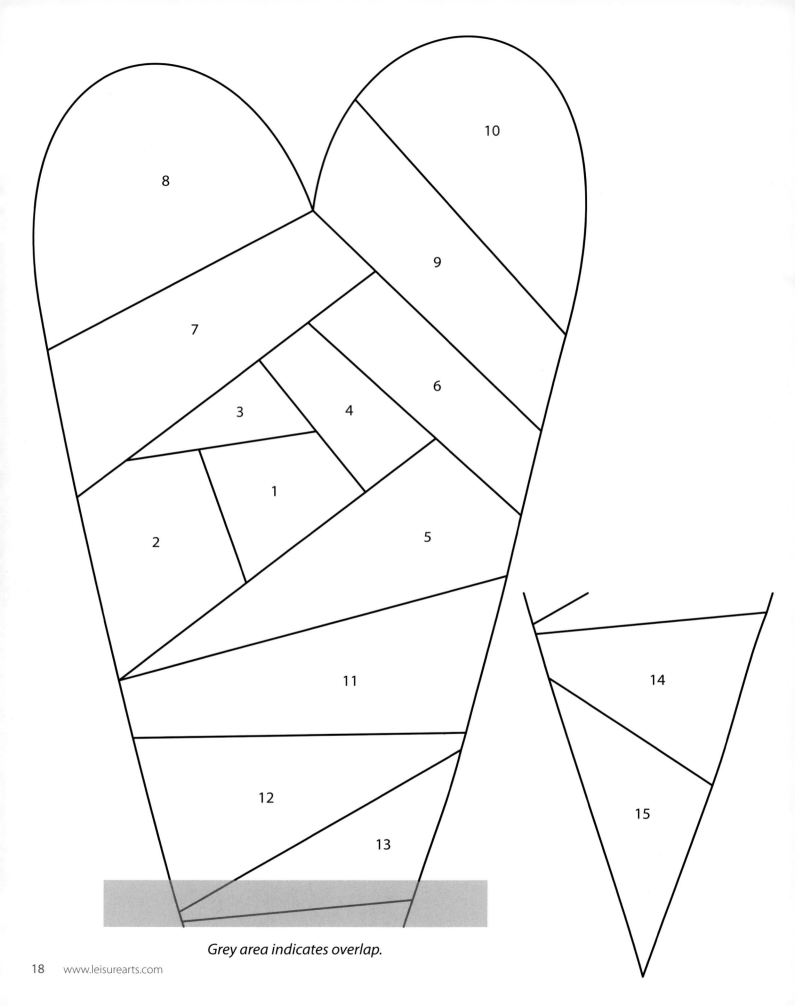

Grey area indicates overlap.

So Beautiful

Finished Size: 19" x 23" (48 x 58 cm)

SHOPPING LIST

Yardage is based on 43"/44" (109 cm/112 cm) wide fabric with a usable width of 40" (102 cm).

- ☐ ⁵/₈ yd (57 cm) of cream print
- ☐ ¹/₈ yd (11 cm) of pink polka dot print
- ☐ ³/₈ yd (34 cm) of small blue and pink floral print
- ☐ ³/₈ yd (34 cm) of large pink floral print with approximately 6" motif
- ☐ ¹/₄ yd (23 cm) of light olive checked print
- ☐ ⁵/₈ yd (57 cm) of fabric for pillow back
- ☐ 1⁵/₈ yds (1.5 m) of muslin

You will also need:

- ☐ 24" x 28" (61 x 71 cm) piece of batting
- ☐ Polyester fiberfill
- ☐ Paper-backed fusible web
- ☐ Stabilizer
- ☐ Tracing paper
- ☐ Hot-iron transfer pen
- ☐ Blue, olive, and gold embroidery floss

CUTTING OUT THE PIECES

*Follow **Rotary Cutting**, page 38, to cut pieces. Measurements listed include seam allowances. Follow **Preparing Fusible Appliqués**, page 39, to cut appliqués. Appliqué patterns do not include seam allowance and are reversed.*

From cream print:

- Cut 1 **large rectangle** 15¹/₂" x 19¹/₂".

From pink polka dot print:

- Cut 2 **top/bottom inner borders** 1¹/₂" x 13¹/₂".
- Cut 2 **side inner borders** 1¹/₂" x 19¹/₂".

From small blue and pink floral print:

- Cut 2 **top/bottom outer borders** 2³/₄" x 15¹/₂".
- Cut 2 **side outer borders** 2³/₄" x 24".

From large pink floral print:

- Cut 1 **small heart** appliqué from pattern on page 24.

From light olive checked print:

- Cut 1 **large heart** appliqué from pattern on pages 22-23.

From fabric for pillow back:

- Cut 2 rectangles 15" x 20" for **pillow back**.

From muslin:

- Cut 1 **large muslin rectangle** 24" x 28".
- Cut 2 **small muslin rectangles** 20" x 24".

MAKING THE PILLOW

*Follow **Piecing**, page 38, **Pressing**, page 39, and **Decorative Stitch Appliqué**, page 39, to make pillow top. Use ¹/₄" seam allowances unless otherwise indicated. Our pillow features machine Blanket Stitch appliqué. Hand embroidered Blanket Stitch with 2 strands of embroidery floss may be substituted. **Hand Stitches** are shown on pages 42-43.*

1. Centering **small heart** on **large heart**, fuse hearts to center of **large rectangle**; appliqué. Trim large rectangle to 13¹/₂" x 17¹/₂".
2. Add **top**, **bottom**, then **side inner borders** to large rectangle. Repeat to add **outer borders**.

3. Using tracing paper and hot-iron transfer pen, transfer words, page 23, and flower design, page 25, to pillow top. Stem Stitch words using 2 strands of blue floss and stems using 2 strands of olive floss. Satin Stitch leaves, then Stem Stitch edges and veins of leaves using 2 strands of olive floss. Make Lazy Daisy Stitches for petals using 2 strands of blue floss, then add French Knots for centers of flowers using 6 strands of gold floss.

4. Layer **large muslin rectangle**, batting, and pillow top (right side up and centered). Follow **Quilting**, page 41, to baste and quilt as desired. Our pillow is machine quilted. The large floral motif is quilted in the ditch and a decorative pattern is added to the background and borders.

5. Trim batting and backing even with edges of pillow top.

6. On each **pillow back** rectangle, press 1 *long* edge $1/4$" to the wrong side; press $1/4$" to the wrong side again and stitch in place.

7. Overlap hemmed edges of pillow back rectangles, right sides facing up, to form 20" x 24" rectangle. Baste pillow back rectangles together at overlap.

8. With right sides facing, pin pillow top and pillow back together. Sew around pillow using $1/2$" **seam allowance**. Remove basting, turn, and press.

9. To make pillow form, sew 2 **small muslin rectangles** together using $1/2$" **seam allowance** and leaving opening for turning. Clip corners, turn and press. Fill with fiberfill; sew opening closed. Insert pillow form in pillow.

Pillow Top Diagram

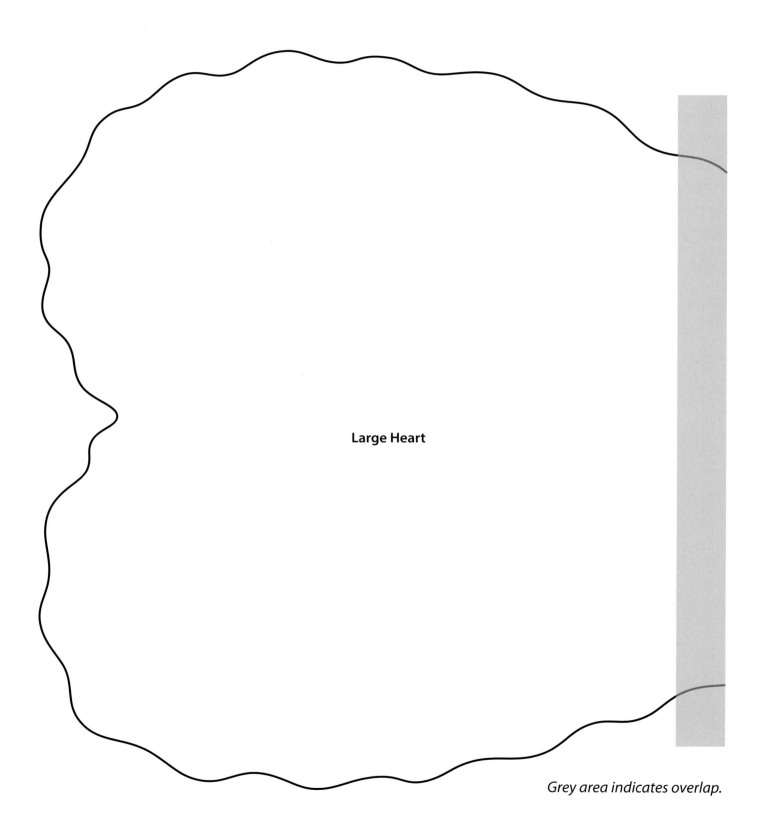

Large Heart

Grey area indicates overlap.

Large Heart

23

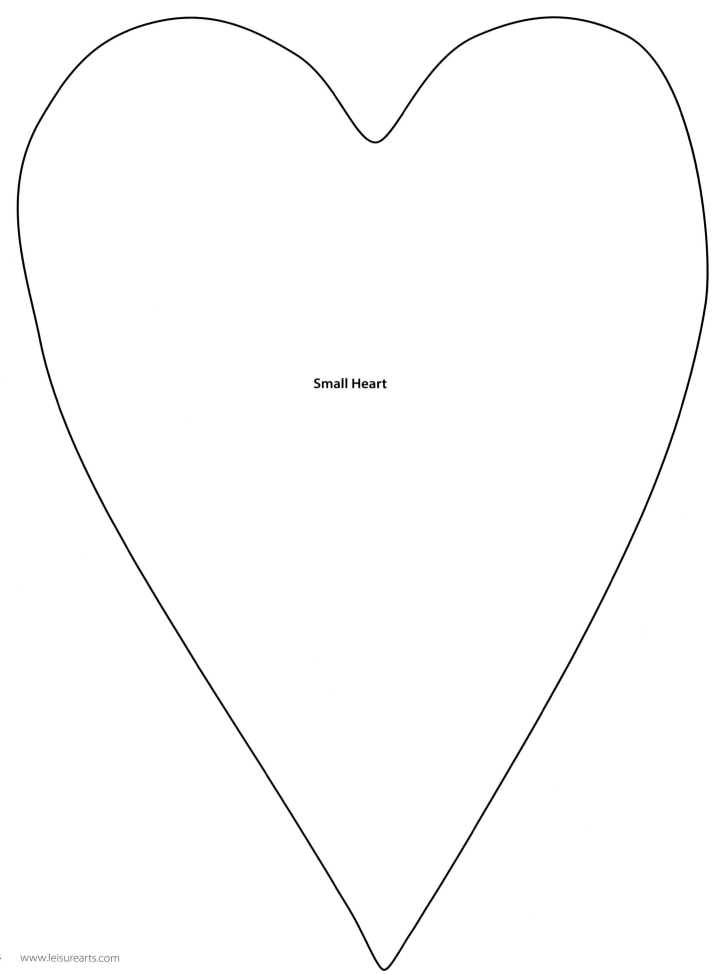

Small Heart

Grey area indicates overlap.

WORK OF MY HANDS

Finished Size: 12" x 17" (30 x 43 cm)

SHOPPING LIST

*Yardage is based on 43"/44"
(109 cm/112 cm) wide fabric with
a usable width of 40" (102 cm).*

- ☐ $^3/_8$ yd (34 cm) of cream print
- ☐ $^1/_4$ yd (23 cm) of tan print
- ☐ $^1/_8$ yd (11 cm) of red polka dot print
- ☐ $^1/_8$ yd (11 cm) of red print
- ☐ Scraps of assorted prints for heart
- ☐ $^3/_8$ yd (34 cm) of fabric for pillow back
- ☐ 1 yd (91 cm) of muslin

You will also need:

- ☐ 17" x 22" (43 x 56 cm) piece of batting
- ☐ Polyester fiberfill
- ☐ Paper-backed fusible web
- ☐ Stabilizer
- ☐ Tracing paper
- ☐ Water- or air-soluble fabric pen
- ☐ Hot-iron transfer pen
- ☐ Black and red embroidery floss
- ☐ Assorted novelty buttons
- ☐ Fine-point marker

CUTTING OUT THE PIECES

*Follow **Rotary Cutting**, page 38, to cut
pieces. Measurements listed include
seam allowances.*

From cream print:
- Cut 1 **large rectangle** $11^1/_2$" x $12^1/_4$".

From tan print:
- Cut 1 **small rectangle** $11^1/_2$" x $5^1/_4$".

From red polka dot print:
- Cut 2 **top/bottom borders** $2^1/_4$" x $9^1/_2$".
- Cut 1 **side border** $2^1/_4$" x 18".

From red print:
- Cut 1 **side border** $2^1/_4$" x 18".

From fabric for pillow back:
- Cut 2 rectangles 12" x 18" for **pillow back**.

From muslin:
- Cut 1 **large muslin rectangle** 17" x 22".
- Cut 2 **small muslin rectangles** 13" x 18".

MAKING PAPER-PIECED APPLIQUÉ HEART

1. Using fine-point marker, trace **pieced heart** pattern, pages 30-31, onto tracing paper.

2. Rough cut a piece of assorted print for heart at least $^1/_2$" larger on all sides than area 1 on traced pattern (foundation). Completely cover area 1 of foundation with fabric, wrong sides together (**Fig. 1**). Pin fabric in place. Fold foundation on line between area 1 and area 2. Trim fabric $^1/_4$" from fold (**Fig. 2**). Unfold foundation.

Fig. 1

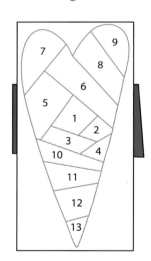

Fig. 2

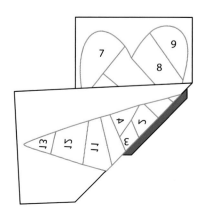

3. Rough cut a piece of another assorted print in the same manner for area 2 on foundation. Match right sides and align 1 edge of piece #2 with trimmed edge of piece #1 (Fig. 3). Turn foundation over to front and pin.

Fig. 3

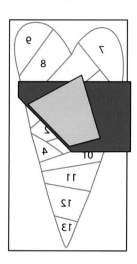

4. Sew along drawn line between areas 1 and 2, extending sewing a few stitches beyond beginning and ending of line (Fig. 4).

Fig. 4

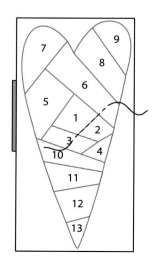

5. Open out piece #2; press. Pin piece #2 to foundation (Fig. 5). Fold foundation on line between area 2 and 3. Trim fabric ¹/₄" from fold. Unfold foundation.

Fig. 5

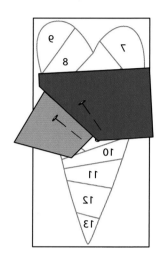

6. Repeat Steps 2-5, adding pieces in numerical order. When adding piece #8, stitch to the inner point of heart *exactly*, and backstitch to reinforce. Add remaining pieces until the foundation is covered. Carefully remove paper foundation.

7. Trace heart shape from **pieced heart** pattern onto paper side of fusible web. Follow manufacturer's instructions to fuse web to wrong side of pieced fabric heart. Trim along traced lines of heart outline.

MAKING THE PILLOW

*Follow **Piecing**, page 38, **Pressing**, page 39, and **Decorative Stitch Appliqué**, page 39, to make pillow top. Use ¹/₄" seam allowances unless otherwise indicated. Our pillow features machine Blanket Stitch appliqué. Hand embroidered Blanket Stitch with 2 strands of embroidery floss may be substituted. **Hand Stitches** are shown on pages 42-43.*

1. Sew **large** and **small rectangles** together to make **Background Unit**.

Background Unit

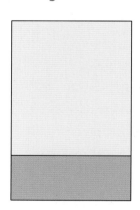

2. Using water- or air-soluble fabric pen, lightly mark a 9" x 14" rectangle in center of Background Unit. *(This will be the finished size of Background Unit. Embroidery and appliqué should fit within drawn rectangle.)* Referring to photo and Pillow Top Diagram, fuse and appliqué heart to Background Unit.

3. Using 2 strands of black floss, add a Running Stitch 1/4" around heart appliqué.

4. Using tracing paper and hot-iron transfer pen, transfer words, page 30, to Background Unit. Backstitch words using 2 strands of red floss. Trim Background Unit to 9 1/2" x 14 1/2" (1/4" outside drawn rectangle).

5. Sew **top**, **bottom**, then **side borders** to Background Unit to complete pillow top.

6. Layer **large muslin rectangle**, batting, and pillow top (right side up and centered). Follow **Quilting**, page 41, to baste and quilt as desired. Our pillow is machine quilted. It has stipple quilting around the words and heart and in the border. The heart pieces are quilted in the ditch.

7. Tie buttons onto pillow top using 6 strands of black floss. Trim batting and backing even with edges of pillow top.

8. On each **pillow back** rectangle, press 1 *short* edge 1/4" to the wrong side; press 1/4" to the wrong side again and stitch in place.

9. Overlap hemmed edges of pillow back rectangles, right sides facing up, to form 13" x 18" rectangle. Baste pillow back rectangles together at overlap.

10. Pin pillow top and pillow back together, right sides facing. Sew around pillow using 1/2" **seam allowance**. Remove basting, turn, and press.

11. To make pillow form, sew 2 **small muslin rectangles** together using 1/2" **seam allowance** and leaving opening for turning. Clip corners, turn and press. Fill with fiberfill; sew opening closed. Insert pillow form in pillow.

Pillow Top Diagram

May

the

work

of

my hands

be a gentle

expression

of the

love

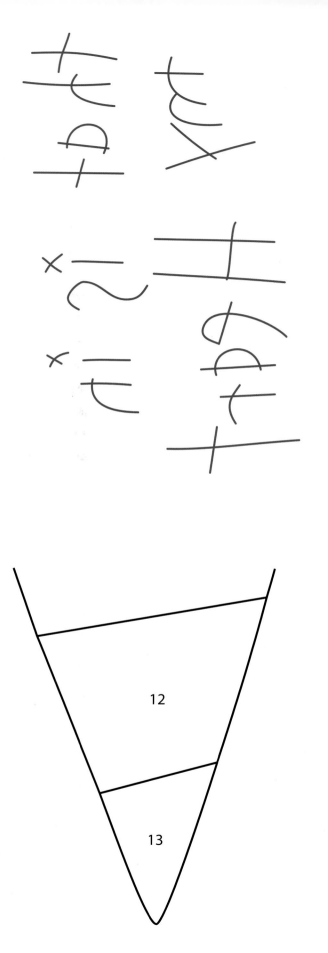

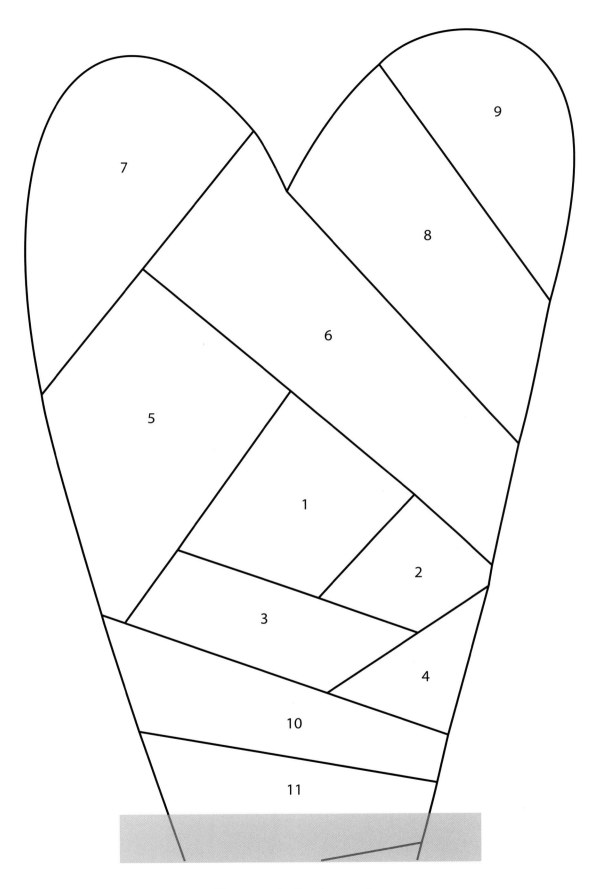

Grey area indicates overlap.

BLESS THIS HOUSE

Finished Size: 20" x 29" (51 x 74 cm)

SHOPPING LIST

Yardage is based on 43"/44" (109 cm/112 cm) wide fabric with a usable width of 40" (102 cm).

☐ ½ yd (46 cm) of cream print

☐ ¼ yd (23 cm) of black print

☐ ½ yd (46 cm) of novelty print

☐ ¼ yd (23 cm) of burgundy print

☐ Scrap of brown print

☐ Scrap of black solid

☐ Scrap of black plaid print

☐ ¾ yd (69 cm) of fabric for pillow back

☐ 2⅛ yds (1.9 m) of muslin

You will also need:

☐ 25" x 34" (64 x 86 cm) piece of batting

☐ Polyester fiberfill

☐ Paper-backed fusible web

☐ Stabilizer

☐ Tracing paper

☐ Water- or air-soluble fabric pen

☐ Hot-iron transfer pen

☐ Black and green embroidery floss

☐ Assorted novelty buttons

CUTTING OUT THE PIECES

*Follow **Rotary Cutting**, page 38, to cut pieces. Measurements listed, except for appliques, include seam allowances. Follow **Preparing Fusible Appliqués**, page 39, to cut appliqués. Roof appliqué pattern is reversed.*

From cream print:

- Cut 1 **large rectangle** 14½" x 23½".

From black print:

- Cut 2 **side inner borders** 1½" x 21½".
- Cut 2 **top/bottom inner borders** 1½" x 14½".

From novelty print:

- Cut 2 **side outer borders** 3¾" x 23½".
- Cut 2 **top/bottom outer borders** 3¾" x 21".

From burgundy print:

- Cut 1 rectangle 5" x 9¼" for **house** appliqué.
- Cut 2 rectangles ¾" x 1½" for **chimney** appliqués.

From brown print:

- Cut 8 rectangles ¾" x 2" for **window** appliqués.

From black solid:

- Cut 1 rectangle 1½" x 3½" for **door** appliqué.

From black plaid:

- Cut 1 **roof** appliqué using pattern on page 35.

From fabric for pillow back:

- Cut 2 rectangles 18" x 21" for **pillow back**.

From muslin:

- Cut 1 **large muslin rectangle** 25" x 34".
- Cut 2 **small muslin rectangles** 21" x 30".

MAKING THE PILLOW

*Follow **Piecing**, page 38, **Pressing**, page 39, and **Decorative Stitch Appliqué**, page 39, to make pillow top. Use ¹/₄" seam allowances unless otherwise indicated. Our pillow features machine Blanket Stitch appliqué. Hand embroidered Blanket Stitch with 2 strands of embroidery floss may be substituted. **Hand Stitches** are shown on pages 42-43.*

1. Using water-soluble pen, lightly mark a 12" x 21" rectangle in center of **large rectangle**. *(This will be the finished size of rectangle. Embroidery and appliqué should fit within drawn rectangle.)* Referring to photo, page 33, and **Pillow Top Diagram**, fuse and appliqué **house**, **chimneys**, **windows**, **door**, and **roof** to large rectangle.

2. Using tracing paper and hot-iron transfer pen, transfer words and vine, pages 36-37, to large rectangle. Backstitch words using 3 strands of black floss. Stem Stitch vine using 2 strands of green floss. Trim large rectangle to 12¹/₂" x 21¹/₂" (¹/₄" outside drawn rectangle).

3. Sew **side**, **top**, then **bottom inner borders** to large rectangle. Repeat to add **outer borders**.

4. Layer **large muslin rectangle**, batting, and pillow top (right side up and centered). Follow **Quilting**, page 41, to baste and quilt as desired. Our pillow is machine quilted. Details are quilted in the appliqués, such as rocks in the chimneys and house using tan thread, panes in the windows using black thread, and panels in the door using tan thread. Decorative quilting fills the cream background, a loop pattern is quilted in the inner border, and straight lines are quilted in the outer border.

5. Sew buttons to pillow top. Trim backing and batting even with edges of pillow top.

6. On each **pillow back** rectangle, press 1 **long** edge ¹/₄" to the wrong side; press ¹/₄" to the wrong side again and stitch in place.

7. Overlap hemmed edges of pillow back rectangles, right sides facing up, to form 21" x 30" rectangle. Baste pillow back rectangles together at overlap.

8. With right sides facing, pin pillow top and pillow back together. Sew around pillow using ¹/₂" **seam allowance**. Remove basting, turn, and press.

9. To make pillow form, sew 2 **small muslin rectangles** together using ¹/₂" **seam allowance** and leaving opening for turning. Clip corners, turn and press. Fill with fiberfill; sew opening closed. Insert pillow form in pillow.

Pillow Top Diagram

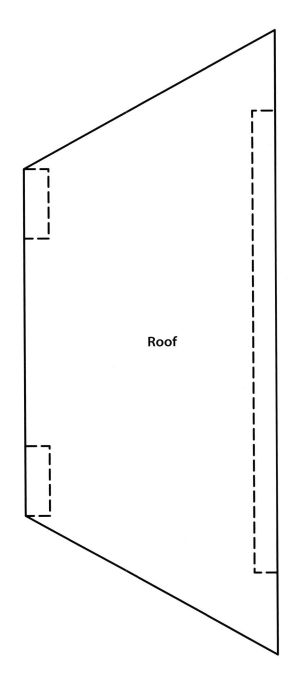

Roof

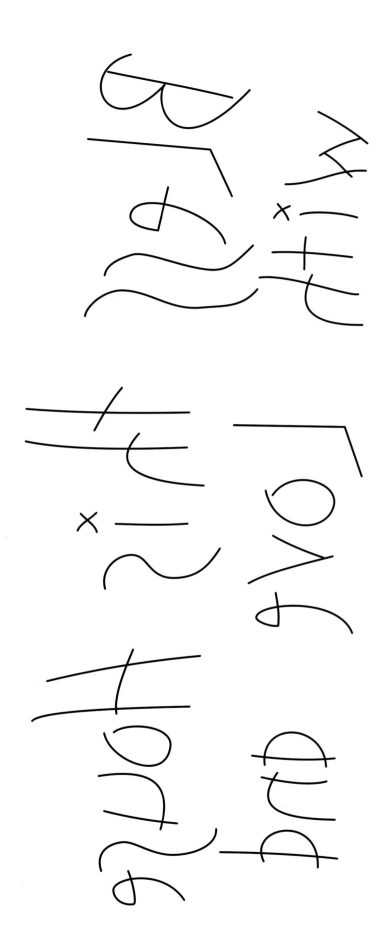

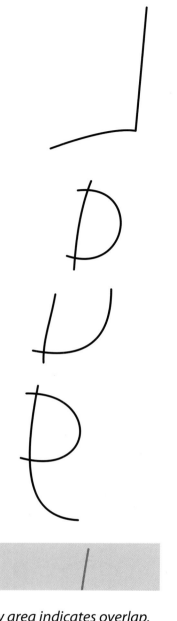

Grey area indicates overlap.

GENERAL INSTRUCTIONS

To make your quilting easier and more enjoyable, we encourage you to carefully read all of the general instructions, study the color photographs, and familiarize yourself with the individual project instructions before beginning a project.

FABRICS

SELECTING FABRICS

Choose high-quality, medium-weight 100% cotton fabrics. All-cotton fabrics hold a crease better, fray less, and are easier to quilt than cotton/polyester blends.

Yardage requirements listed for each project are based on 43"/44" (109 cm/112 cm) wide fabric with a "usable" width of 40" (102 cm) after shrinkage and trimming selvages. Actual usable width will probably vary slightly from fabric to fabric. Our recommended yardage lengths should be adequate for occasional re-squaring of fabric when many cuts are required.

PREPARING FABRICS

We recommend that all fabrics be washed, dried, and pressed before cutting. If fabrics are not pre-washed, washing finished pillow will cause shrinkage and give it a more "antiqued" look and feel. Bright and dark colors, which may run, should always be washed before cutting. After washing and drying fabric, fold lengthwise with wrong sides together and matching selvages.

ROTARY CUTTING

Rotary cutting has brought speed and accuracy to quiltmaking by allowing quilters to easily cut strips of fabric and then cut those strips into smaller pieces.

- Place fabric on work surface with fold closest to you.
- Cut all strips from selvage-to-selvage width of fabric unless otherwise indicated in project instructions.
- Square left edge of fabric using rotary cutter and rulers (**Figs. 1-2**).

Fig. 1

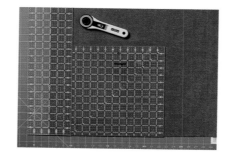

Fig. 2

- To cut each strip required for a project, place ruler over cut edge of fabric, aligning desired marking on ruler with cut edge; make cut (**Fig. 3**).

Fig. 3

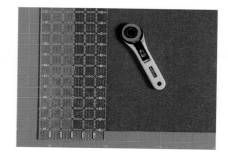

PIECING

Precise cutting, followed by accurate piecing, will ensure that all pieces of pillow top fit together well.

- Set sewing machine stitch length for approximately 11 stitches per inch.
- Use neutral-colored general-purpose sewing thread (not quilting thread) in needle and in bobbin.
- An accurate $1/4$" seam allowance is **essential**. Presser feet that are $1/4$" wide are available for most sewing machines.

- When piecing, always place pieces right sides together and match raw edges; pin if necessary.
- Chain piecing saves time and will usually result in more accurate piecing.
- Trim away points of seam allowances that extend beyond edges of sewn pieces.

Sewing Across Seam Intersections
When sewing across intersection of 2 seams, place pieces right sides together and match seams exactly, making sure seam allowances are pressed in opposite directions (**Fig. 4**).

Fig. 4

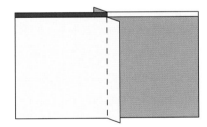

PRESSING
- Use steam iron set on "Cotton" for all pressing.
- Press after sewing each seam.
- Seam allowances are almost always pressed to 1 side, usually toward darker fabric. However, to reduce bulk it may occasionally be necessary to press seam allowances toward the lighter fabric or even to press them open.

- To prevent dark fabric seam allowance from showing through light fabric, trim darker seam allowance slightly narrower than lighter seam allowance.
- To press long seams without curving or other distortion, lay strips across width of the ironing board.

APPLIQUÉ
PREPARING FUSIBLE APPLIQUÉS
Patterns for fused appliqués are printed in reverse to enable you to use our speedy method of preparing appliqués. White or light-colored fabrics may need to be lined with fusible interfacing before applying fusible web to prevent darker fabrics from showing through.

1. Place paper-backed fusible web, web side down, over appliqué pattern. Use a pencil to trace pattern, including any detail lines, onto paper side of web as many times as indicated in project instructions for a single fabric. Repeat for additional patterns and fabrics.
2. Follow manufacturer's instructions to fuse traced patterns to wrong side of fabrics. Do not remove paper backing. (*Note: Some pieces may be given as measurements, such as a 2" x 4" rectangle, instead of drawn patterns. Fuse web to wrong side of the fabrics indicated for these pieces.*)

3. Use scissors to cut out appliqué pieces along traced lines; use rotary cutting equipment to cut out appliqué pieces given as measurements.
4. Remove paper backing from appliqué pieces.

DECORATIVE STITCH APPLIQUÉ
Some sewing machines are capable of a Blanket Stitch. Refer to your Owner's Manual for machine set-up. If your machine does not have this stitch, try any of the decorative stitches your machine has until you are satisfied with the look.

1. Thread sewing machine and bobbin with general-purpose thread.
2. Arrange appliqué pieces on background fabric as described in project instructions. Fuse appliqués in place.
3. Attach an open-toe presser foot. Select far right needle position and needle down (if your machine has these features).
4. Pin a stabilizer, such as paper or any of the commercially available products, on wrong side of background fabric before stitching appliqués in place.
5. Begin by stitching 2 or 3 stitches in place (drop feed dogs or set stitch length at 0) to anchor thread.

6. Most of the decorative stitch should be done on the appliqué with the right edges of the stitch falling at the very outside edge of the appliqué. Stitch over all exposed raw edges of appliqué pieces.

7. (*Note: Dots on (Figs. 5-10) indicate where to leave needle in fabric when pivoting.*) Always stopping with needle down in background fabric, refer to Fig. 5 to stitch outside points like tips of leaves. Stop one stitch short of point. Raise presser foot. Pivot project slightly, lower presser foot, and make an angled Stitch 1. Take next stitch, stop at point, and pivot so Stitch 2 will be perpendicular to point. Pivot slightly to make Stitch 3. Continue stitching.

Fig. 5

8. For outside corners (Fig. 6), stitch to the corner, stopping with the needle in background fabric. Raise presser foot. Pivot project, lower presser foot, and take an angled stitch. Raise presser foot. Pivot project, lower presser foot and stitch adjacent side.

Fig. 6

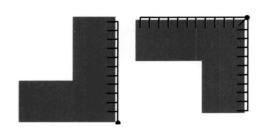

9. For inside corners (Fig. 7), stitch to the corner, taking the last bite at corner and stopping with the needle down in background fabric. Raise presser foot. Pivot project, lower presser foot, and take an angled stitch. Raise presser foot. Pivot project, lower presser foot and stitch adjacent side.

Fig. 7

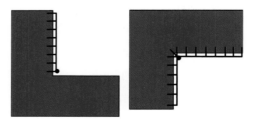

10. When stitching outside curves (Fig. 8), stop with needle down in background fabric. Raise presser foot and pivot project as needed. Lower presser foot and continue stitching, pivoting as often as necessary to follow curve. Small circles may require pivoting between each stitch.

Fig. 8

11. When stitching inside curves (Fig. 9), stop with needle down in background fabric. Raise presser foot and pivot project as needed. Lower presser foot and continue stitching, pivoting as often as necessary to follow curve.

Fig. 9

12. When stopping stitching, use a lock stitch to sew 5 or 6 stitches in place or use a needle to pull threads to wrong side of background fabric (**Fig. 10**); knot, then trim ends.

Fig. 10

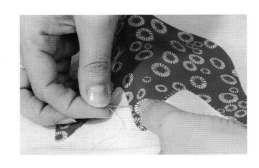

13. Carefully tear away stabilizer.

QUILTING

Quilting holds the 3 layers (top, batting, and backing) of the pillow top together. Because marking, layering, and quilting are interrelated and may be done in different orders depending on circumstances, please read entire Quilting section, pages 41-42, before beginning project.

MARKING QUILTING LINES

Quilting lines may be marked using fabric marking pencils, chalk markers, or water- or air-soluble pens.

Simple quilting designs may be marked with chalk or chalk pencil after basting. A small area may be marked, then quilted, before moving to next area to be marked. Intricate designs should be marked before basting using a more durable marker.

Caution: Some marks may be permanently set by pressing. **Test** different markers **on scrap fabric** to find one that marks clearly and can be thoroughly removed.

A wide variety of precut quilting stencils, as well as entire books of quilting patterns, are available. Using a stencil makes it easier to mark intricate or repetitive designs.

To make a stencil from a pattern, center template plastic over pattern and use a permanent marker to trace pattern onto plastic. Use a craft knife with single or double blade to cut channels along traced lines (**Fig. 11**).

Fig. 11

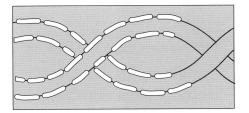

CHOOSING THE BATTING

The appropriate batting will make quilting easier. For fine hand quilting, choose low-loft batting. All cotton or cotton/polyester blend battings work well for machine quilting because the cotton helps "grip" pillow top layers.

Types of batting include cotton, polyester, cotton/polyester blend, wool, cotton/wool blend, and silk. When selecting batting, refer to package labels for characteristics and care instructions.

ASSEMBLING THE PILLOW TOP LAYERS

1. Examine wrong side of pillow top closely; trim any seam allowances and clip any threads that may show through front of the pillow top. Press pillow top, being careful not to "set" any marked quilting lines.

2. Place muslin backing on flat surface. Use masking tape to tape edges of backing to surface. Place batting on top of backing. Smooth batting gently, being careful not to stretch or tear. Center pillow top *right* side up on batting.

3. Use 1" rustproof safety pins to "pin-baste" all layers together, spacing pins approximately 4" apart. Begin at center and work toward outer edges to secure all layers. If possible, place pins away from areas that will be quilted, although pins may be removed as needed when quilting.

MACHINE QUILTING METHODS

Use general-purpose thread in bobbin. Do not use quilting thread. Thread the needle of machine with general-purpose thread or transparent monofilament thread to make quilting blend with pillow top fabrics. Use decorative thread, such as a metallic or contrasting-color general-purpose thread, to make quilting lines stand out more.

Straight Line Quilting

The term "straight-line" is somewhat deceptive, since curves (especially gentle ones) as well as straight lines can be stitched with this technique.

1. Set stitch length for 6-10 stitches per inch and attach walking foot to sewing machine.

2. Determine which section of pillow top will have longest continuous quilting line, oftentimes area from center top to center bottom.

3. Begin stitching on longest quilting line, using very short stitches for the first 1/4" to "lock" quilting. Stitch across pillow top, using 1 hand on each side of walking foot to slightly spread fabric and to guide fabric through machine. Lock stitches at end of quilting line.

4. Continue machine quilting, stitching longer quilting lines first to stabilize pillow top before moving on to other areas.

Free Motion Quilting

Free motion quilting may be free form or may follow a marked pattern.

1. Attach darning foot to sewing machine and lower or cover feed dogs.

2. Position pillow top under darning foot. Holding top thread, take 1 stitch and pull bobbin thread to top of pillow top. To "lock" beginning of quilting line, hold top and bobbin threads while making 3 to 5 stitches in place.

3. Use 1 hand on each side of darning foot to slightly spread fabric and to move fabric through the machine. Even stitch length is achieved by using smooth, flowing hand motion and steady machine speed. Slow machine speed and fast hand movement will create long stitches. Fast machine speed and slow hand movement will create short stitches. Move pillow top sideways, back and forth, in a circular motion, or in a random motion to create desired designs; do not rotate pillow top. Lock stitches at end of each quilting line.

HAND STITCHES
BACK STITCH

Come up at 1, go down at 2, and come up at 3 (Fig. 12). Continue working as shown in Fig. 13. Length of stitches may be varied as desired.

Fig. 12

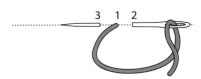

Fig. 13

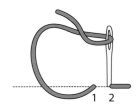

BLANKET STITCH

Come up at 1, go down at 2, and come up at 3, keeping thread below point of needle (Fig. 14). Continue working as shown in Fig. 15.

Fig. 14 **Fig. 15**

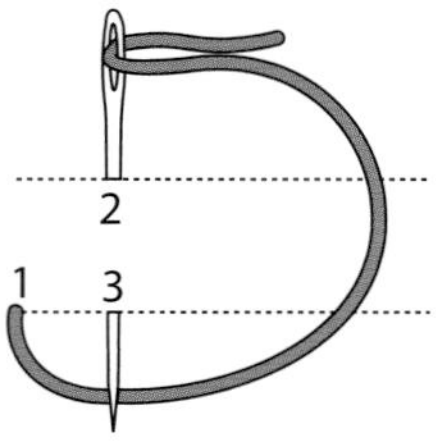

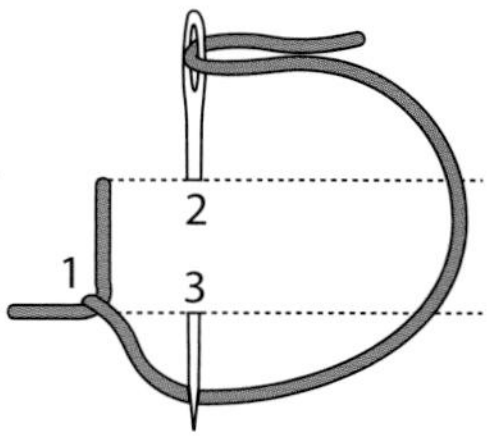

FRENCH KNOT

Follow Figs. 16-19 to complete French Knots. Come up at 1. Wrap thread twice around needle and insert needle at 2, holding end of thread with non-stitching fingers. Tighten knot then pull needle through, holding floss until it must be released.

Fig. 16   Fig. 17

Fig. 18   Fig. 19

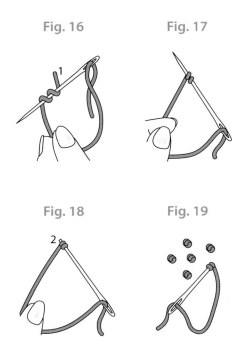

LAZY DAISY STITCH

Come up at 1 and go down again at 1 to form a loop. Come up at 2. Keeping loop below point of needle (Fig. 20), go down at 3 to anchor loop (Fig. 21).

Fig. 20   Fig. 21

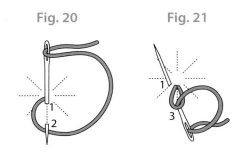

RUNNING STITCH

The running stitch consists of a series of straight stitches with the stitch length equal to the space between stitches. Come up at 1, go down at 2, and come up at 3 (Fig. 22).

Fig. 22

SATIN STITCH

Come up at 1, go down at 2, and come up at 3. Continue until area is filled (Fig. 23).

Fig. 23

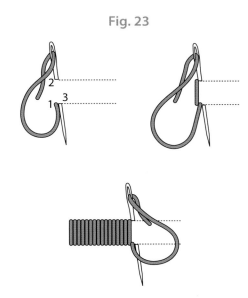

STEM STITCH

Come up at 1. Keeping thread below the stitching line, go down at 2 and come up at 3. Go down at 4 and come up at 5 (Fig. 24).

Fig. 24

MEET THE DESIGNER

Tricia Cribbs of Turning Twenty® (formerly FriendFolks) has been a top-selling quilt designer and lecturer for more than 20 years. Creating impressive quilts that are surprisingly simple to piece and quick to complete is her signature style. Tricia finishes her quilts with beautiful freehand machine quilting that resembles the intricate hand stitching found on antique quilts.

More information may be found on her website, TurningTwenty.com.

Metric Conversion Chart

Inches x 2.54 = centimeters (cm)	Yards x .9144 = meters (m)
Inches x 25.4 = millimeters (mm)	Yards x 91.44 = centimeters (cm)
Inches x .0254 = meters (m)	Centimeters x .3937 = inches (")
	Meters x 1.0936 = yards (yd)

Standard Equivalents

1/8"	3.2 mm	0.32 cm	1/8 yard	11.43 cm	0.11 m
1/4"	6.35 mm	0.635 cm	1/4 yard	22.86 cm	0.23 m
3/8"	9.5 mm	0.95 cm	3/8 yard	34.29 cm	0.34 m
1/2"	12.7 mm	1.27 cm	1/2 yard	45.72 cm	0.46 m
5/8"	15.9 mm	1.59 cm	5/8 yard	57.15 cm	0.57 m
3/4"	19.1 mm	1.91 cm	3/4 yard	68.58 cm	0.69 m
7/8"	22.2 mm	2.22 cm	7/8 yard	80 cm	0.8 m
1"	25.4 mm	2.54 cm	1 yard	91.44 cm	0.91 m

Production Team: Technical Writer – Frances Huddleston; Associate Editor – Lisa Lancaster; Editorial Writer – Susan Frantz Wiles; Senior Graphic Artist – Lora Puls; Graphic Artist – Cailen Cochren.